BENCHMARKING BASICS
Looking for a Better Way

James G. Patterson

A FIFTY-MINUTE™ SERIES BOOK

CRISP PUBLICATIONS, INC.
Menlo Park, California

BENCHMARKING BASICS
Looking for a Better Way

James G. Patterson

CREDITS
Managing Editor: **Kathleen Barcos**
Editor: **Kay Keppler**
Typesetting: **ExecuStaff**
Cover Design: **Carol Harris**
Artwork: **Ralph Mapson**

Distribution to the U.S. Trade:

National Book Network, Inc.
4720 Boston Way
Lanham, MD 20706
1-800-462-6420

Distribution to the Canadian Trade:

Raincoast Books
8680 Cambie Street
Vancouver, B.C.
V6P 6M9
604-323-7100
800-663-5714

Copyright © 1996 by Crisp Publications, Inc.

Printed in the United States of America by Bawden Printing Company.

Library of Congress Catalog Card Number 95-69642
Patterson, James G.
Benchmarking Basics
ISBN 1-56052-356-5

This book is printed on recyclable paper with soy ink.

PREFACE

Benchmarking is a way to determine the processes of the best people and organizations in any field and apply their methods to your company. Robert C. Camp, benchmarking guru of Xerox, credits benchmarking with helping Xerox become more competitive worldwide. Many other organizations, big and small, manufacturing and service, public and private, have learned the competitive advantage benchmarking brings. Benchmarking will open your eyes to new ideas from similar and dissimilar organizations and show you how doing things differently can improve performance.

☐ Do you want to improve your performance?

☐ Do you want to put more emphasis on learning what really matters to your customers?

☐ Do you want to improve your organization's processes?

☐ Do you want to learn a technique that can increase your organization's productivity by one-third?

If you answered yes to any of these questions, this book is for you.

James G. Patterson

James G. Patterson

ABOUT THIS BOOK

Benchmarking Basics will give you a thorough understanding of what benchmarking is, why you should want to do it for your unit or organization, and how to plan, conduct and use a benchmarking study.

Benchmarking is a remarkably easy tool to use. It will not replace the total quality management effort, but it will help it.

By setting up a benchmarking program, you will be opening your eyes and ears to other, better ways of doing things. This is often a humbling experience for people and organizations who think they already know it all; moreover, you might learn how to improve from people and organizations who work quite differently from you.

Benchmarking Basics can be used effectively in a number of ways. Here are some possibilities:

► **Individual Study.** Because the book is self-instructional, all that is needed is a quiet place, some time and a pencil. Completing the activities and exercises will provide valuable feedback, as well as practical ideas for improving your business.

► **Workshops and Seminars.** This book is ideal for use during, or as pre-assigned reading prior to, a workshop or seminar. With the basics in hand, the quality and participation will improve. More time can be spent practicing concept extensions and applications during the program.

► **College Programs.** Thanks to the format, brevity and low cost, this book is ideal for short courses and extension programs.

There are other possibilities that depend on the objectives of the user. One thing is certain: Even after it has been read, this book will serve as excellent reference material that can easily be reviewed.

ABOUT THE AUTHOR

Jim Patterson has been a trainer, speaker and consultant since 1980. His specialties are *quality* (ISO 9000, TQM, Team Building, Customer Service, Benchmarking) and *communication* (effective writing, presentation skills, conflict management, negotiating, leadership).

Jim has written articles on quality and communication for *Management World, The Toastmaster Magazine, Sound Management,* and the *Military Intelligence Magazine.* His ASTD "Info-Line" book, *Fundamentals of Leadership,* was its February 1994 selection. Jim also wrote the Crisp Publication book *ISO 9000: Worldwide Quality Standard.* He is an active member of the American Society for Quality Control (ASQC) and Association for Quality and Participation (AQP). Jim is an Arizona Quality award auditor.

Jim received his MA in organizational communication from Eastern Michigan University and his BA in journalism and international relations from the University of Arizona. He has done advanced graduate work in business, communication, and adult education at the University of Arizona. In addition, Jim holds an ASQC Certified Quality Auditor (CQA) Certificate and a Registrar Accreditation Board (RAB) Approved ISO 9000 Lead Auditor Training Certificate.

You can reach Jim Patterson through:

The Cogent Communicator
9571 East Caldwell Drive
Tucson, Arizona 85747-9218
(520) 574-9353   FAX: (520) 574-0620
E-mail Address: Cogent @ indirect.com

ACKNOWLEDGMENTS

I'd like to thank the following people for their help on this book: Marni Patterson, my loving wife, for her help on spelling and readability; Alex Dely, Tucson Transatlantic Trade and Chapman College, for leading me to some excellent sources; the research staffs at the American Society for Quality Control and Association for Quality and Participation for providing superb bibliographies.

Dedication

This book is dedicated to my mother, Aniceta Patterson, and my late father, James G. "Doc" Patterson. Products of the Depression and a Michigan upbringing, they both tried to teach me the value of learning and questioning to improve, one of the benefits of benchmarking.

CONTENTS

INTRODUCTION

We've all done benchmarking before. You've probably admired other people, how they dress, speak or act. You've studied them, asked questions of others, may have even interviewed the person to find out how he or she does it. When we want to learn more about a subject, we read magazines and books and spend money and time on tapes and classes.

The essence of benchmarking is measuring, managing and satisfying customer requirements and expectations, assessing your strengths and weaknesses, finding and studying the best practices wherever you find them, and adapting what you learn to your circumstances.

Quality-enhancing benchmarking is sweeping the world. You're not a Fortune 500 company? No problem. Benchmarking is easy enough for all kinds of companies and individuals to use.

S E C T I O N

I

Benchmarking: What About It?

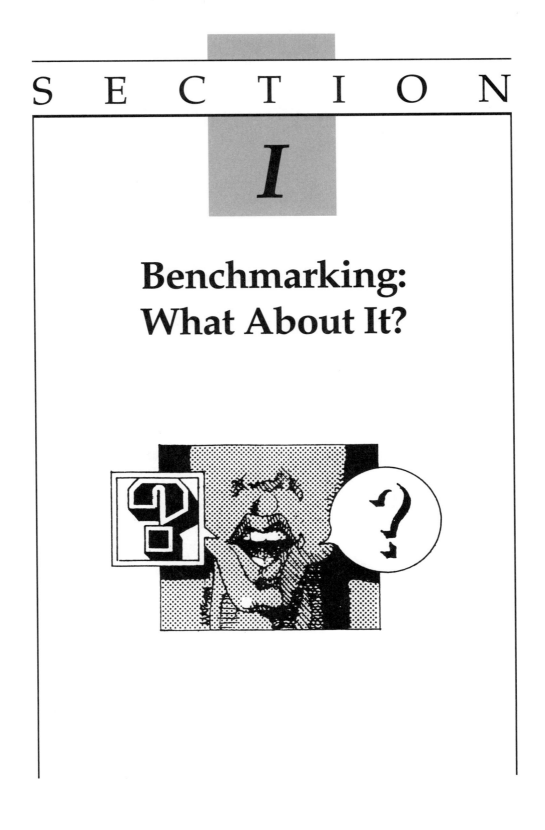

OBJECTIVES

Find and use the best practices in your industry! Benchmarking is nothing more than copying what works. Benefits of successful benchmarking include: meeting customer requirements, setting achievable goals, developing accurate measures of productivity, becoming competitive, and adapting the best industry-wide practices.

After reading this book, you will:

❏ Know what benchmarking is all about.

❏ Discover the benefits to benchmarking.

❏ Know where to find benchmarking data.

❏ Learn the requirements for benchmarking.

❏ Find out what kinds of benchmarking are available.

❏ Decide whether to hire a consultant or do benchmarking yourself.

❏ Come away with an action plan.

WHAT IS BENCHMARKING?

The biggest room in the world is the room for change.
—Anonymous

Benchmarking needn't be a mysterious process. Any person or organization can and should do it. At the core of benchmarking is the concept of learning and sharing. By comparing work practices with others, you may gain valuable information that you can adapt to your own situation.

You'll find best practices not only in your industry, but in places you may have thought had no relationship to you whatsoever. Moreover, you can benchmark just about everything, from machine downtime to employee overtime to delivery time. Every company must grapple with these issues, and every manager can learn from others' experiences.

Benchmarking is a useful quality tool that will help your company continually improve its processes by learning how others do it. To benchmark, you first evaluate your own operation's processes to identify weaknesses and strengths; then you must identify, study and adapt from others who may be doing it better.

The word benchmarking originally was a land surveyor's term. In that context, a benchmark was a distinctive mark made on a rock, building or wall, and it was used as a reference point in determining the position or altitude in topographical surveys and tidal observation. Today a benchmark is a sighting point to make measurements; a standard against which others could be measured.

You can attribute some of the recent popularity of benchmarking to the Malcolm Baldrige National Quality Award, which requires all company entries to benchmark. Another, perhaps more powerful reason to benchmark is to keep up with world-class competition.

Benchmarking is most often used to identify the best organizational practices, but you can also use it to improve performance by studying what your competitors know and the rate at which they learn it. Research shows that people like to know where they stand with managers, with the company as a whole and with their contemporaries. You can benchmark with others in your own company to take advantage of information easily available, or you can benchmark with individuals in other companies to give yourself and others a more complete picture of what is considered the best.

Understanding Benchmarking: The First Steps

One of the first steps in understanding benchmarking is understanding what you do and why you do it. List two processes you could improve, based on your own internal measures or feedback from customers.

#1 _____

#2 _____

For each of the two processes you listed above, think of three organizations you could benchmark against that do that process. Do not restrict yourself by listing only organizations in the same business you are in.

PROCESS #1: _____

Possible Organizations to Benchmark:

#1 _____

#2 _____

#3 _____

PROCESS #2: _____

Possible Organizations to Benchmark:

#1 _____

#2 _____

#3 _____

If you are having a bit of trouble thinking of organizations at this point, don't worry. Coming up are some examples of benchmarking within and outside of various industries.

WHAT IS BENCHMARKING? (continued)

To be able to learn wherever you find a better way of doing things means you will have to fight the biggest obstacle to organizational progress: self-satisfaction. It takes a great deal of ego-suppression and an open mind to look closely at how you do what you do and ask, "But how can we be *better?*"

Goodlow Suttler, a general manager at Analog Devices, was one of 25 people who created the Center for Quality Management in Boston. Suttler says he had thought that Analog operated well until he saw how American Baldrige Award winners and Japanese Deming Award winners operated. "The practices we saw in both Japan and the United States were incredibly motivating and moving. After I came back, I had enough to propel myself for several years."

One of the great values of benchmarking is that if you learn nothing else, at least you've taken a good, hard look at how you do business.

THE ORIGINS OF BENCHMARKING

Who was the very first benchmarker? Possibly the second person to light a fire is humanity's first benchmarker. The way it worked: The second fire starter watched the first fire starter and then borrowed the practice.

Xerox introduced the concept of benchmarking to present-day corporations in 1979. In no time, it seemed that the idea of improving corporate and organizational improvement by collecting and adapting the best practices of others started what some call a new quality science.

Today, many organizations have dedicated benchmarking departments led by managers who specialize in it. Benchmarking is an easy process that any organization can learn and inexpensively use. While some companies report spending more than $1 million annually on benchmarking, smaller organizations spend far less. A recent International Benchmarking Clearinghouse (IBC) membership survey finds that one to two days of training in benchmarking should be adequate preparation for most people. More than 80% of the respondents say benchmarking study leaders need two or fewer days of training.

WHAT WILL BENCHMARKING HELP YOUR COMPANY ACHIEVE?

WHY USE BENCHMARKING?

Benchmarking can help companies do two things.

#1 *It helps companies focus on significant improvements rather than incremental improvements and helps identify real-life targets.*

#2 *Benchmarking provides a measurement system. Figuring out what to benchmark moves you to measure your own processes.*

International competition for domestic markets means that companies must now, more than ever, emphasize quality. One way to ensure quality and effective process control is to benchmark—measure and test standard operational procedure against new methods.

List a few key points and benefits that describe benchmarking for your boss, coworkers and employees.

▶ _____

_____

▶ _____

_____

▶ _____

_____

▶ _____

_____

DEFINE YOUR BENCHMARKING OBJECTIVES

What is the first thing you ought to do before taking on a benchmarking project? You have to define your objectives. Why are you benchmarking? What process do you want to improve? By how much?

Many organizations start out on a learning experience like benchmarking thinking their objective is to improve the bottom line (make more money). Certainly, that is what companies are in business for: to increase stockholder equity. Although it may be hard for companies that are new and struggling (or even more "mature" companies stuck in old ways of thinking), money and profits actually are a *result* of the effective use and application of the information you'll get through benchmarking. Customers can tell when companies are in it only for the money. For long-term success and profit, you have to be in it for the customer. Someone once said, "Do what you love and the money will follow." Wise advice for companies, too.

Sophisticated learning organizations know that they'll never know enough, they'll never be good enough, and that they can learn from others, no matter what business the others are in. They know that customers' wants and needs change and the environment they do business in changes as well. So they must be willing to change. Benchmarking can help adjust to these changes.

Your benchmarking study must have clear, accurate objectives based on customer requirements. Make sure you know what your customers (or potential customers) want before you do this. You should be polling customers regularly through phone surveys, mail surveys, focus group studies, site visits, or a combination of all of these methods. Successful benchmarking companies use the following criteria to help them decide on a suitable benchmarking objective:

- ✔ Is it of interest to our customers?
- ✔ Does it focus on a critical business need?
- ✔ Is it in an area where additional information could influence plans and actions?
- ✔ Is it significant in cost or key nonfinancial indicators?

DEFINE YOUR BENCHMARKING OBJECTIVES (continued)

So why should *you* benchmark? Use this checklist to come up with your benchmarking objectives.

We want to use benchmarking to improve our

☐ Distribution system

☐ Warehousing

☐ Payroll system

☐ New product introduction cycle

☐ How we schedule projects

☐ Product design process

☐ Company's cost management system

☐ Human resource staffing processes

☐ Customer service reaction process

☐ Accounting practices

OTHERS: _____

_____

_____

_____

Xerox: A Case in Point

In 1979, Japan's Canon, Inc. introduced a midsize copier for less than $10,000, or less than it cost Xerox to make a similar machine. Xerox first assumed Canon could do this because it priced the product below fair market value to buy market share, but Xerox engineers showed that Canon could sell its product cheaper because Canon was more efficient. Xerox took more than a year to decide to change their ways to compete. Xerox decided to benchmark Canon's processes with the objective of reducing costs. It was Xerox's turn-around through benchmarking that started the movement in the United States.

From 1980 to 1985, Xerox adapted Japanese techniques to cut its unit production costs in half and slash inventory costs more than 60 percent. Since then, the Xerox share of the U.S. copier market has climbed 80 percent to almost 18 percent.

Everything Xerox does centers on surpassing customer expectations. Their Customer Satisfaction Measurement System, in which more than 200,000 Xerox customers have been polled every year for the last decade, has resulted in the company improving its number of highly satisfied customers by more than 38 percent.

The amount of benchmarking Xerox does has vastly increased since 1984, when they benchmarked only 14 performance elements. Now more than 240 elements are benchmarked and the ultimate target for each attribute is the level of performance a world-class leader achieves, regardless of industry.

DEFINE YOUR BENCHMARKING OBJECTIVES (continued)

Xerox Benchmarking Partners

PARTNER	PROCESS
► American Express	billing and collections
► American Hospital Supply	automated inventory control
► Florida Light and Power	overall quality processes
► Ford Motor Company	manufacturing floor layout
► General Electric	robotics
► L.L. Bean	warehouse operations
► Mary Kay Cosmetics	warehouse and distribution efficiency
► Cummins Engine Company	world-class daily production schedules
► Westinghouse	Baldrige Award application process, warehouse controls, bar coding

The Xerox turnaround did not go unnoticed. Inquiries came in from a variety of other companies. By the mid-1980s, benchmarking was leading to improvements at AT&T, Hewlett-Packard, and many other organizations.

OTHER SUCCESSFUL BENCHMARKERS

COMPANY	PROCESS BENCHMARKED	METHODS USED	RESULTS
L. L. BEAN	• Stocking/packing stations • Packing efficiency	• Listened to workers • Plotted packers' movements on flowcharts	• Moved high-volume items close to packing stations
MOTOROLA	• Manufacturing quality of consumer electronics	• Sent benchmarking team to Japan to study their auto manufacturing facilities	• Lowered the defect rate and reduced costs
XEROX	• Logistics and distribution • Warehouse productivity	• Examined L.L. Bean's fulfillment methods	• Gained over 5% in warehouse productivity
KPMG PETE MARWICK	• Expediting word-processing changes in documents	• Analyzed supermarket express lane checkout practices	• Established express lines • Improved internal customer satisfaction • Improved cycle time
SOUTHWEST AIRLINES	• Refueling and after-flight servicing at docks	• Analyzed race car pit-stop crews' processes	• Improved turn-around time and efficiency
CHRYSLER	• Assembly line problem-solving processes	• Looked into L.L. Bean's worker-level problem-solving process	• Speeded up the assembly line by having workers solve line problems
MOTOROLA	• Cycle time between order receipt and product delivery	• Studied Domino Pizza's order and delivery procedures	• Reduced cycle time
CONVEX COMPUTERS	• Routine maintenance and repairs	• Benchmarked Disney World's fixed patterns for routine maintenance chores • Empowered workers to make on-the-spot decisions	• Reduced electrical breakdowns by 80%, which saved millions of dollars

STATOIL: SUCCESSFUL BENCHMARKING IN EUROPE

Benchmarking in Europe is not as developed as it is in the United States, but it is coming, especially among the big industries. Some countries, such as the United Kingdom, France, and Holland, are actively taking it up as part of their continuous improvement process. A few organizations in Sweden are using benchmarking as well.

Leading benchmarking experts consider Statoil Group of Stavanger, Norway, to be that country's benchmarking leader. Bjorn Bentsen, Statoil Corporate Quality Manager, is active in promoting benchmarking throughout Norway. In fact, Bentsen says one of the biggest challenges facing the company is finding benchmarking partners close to home.

Statoil's top management asked Bentsen to study benchmarking to see if there was any value in it for Statoil. They knew benchmarking was popular in the United States, so they visited the benchmarking operations at world leaders like AT&T, Xerox, and Amoco.

After visiting U.S. benchmarkers, Statoil's upper management decided to join forces with I.B.C. They held a seminar for top management to introduce benchmarking. From this seminar, the company was able to introduce the benchmarking process to everyone in the company and to create benchmarking guidelines for every employee.

Why benchmark? Company leaders believe benchmarking helps Statoil become a "learning organization," and is one of the key tools they use to improve productivity and internal and external customer satisfaction.

A European Benchmarking Success Story

Statoil's objectives for their first benchmarking project were:

1. **Improve Productivity**

2. **Improve Customer Satisfaction**

3. **Gain Competence and Experience Benchmarking**

Bentsen and other management leaders decided to study key elements of the petroleum industry's supply chain for drill casing, which were costing Statoil $65 million U.S. per year.

Statoil started with a full-time project manager and a steering committee of six people. They analyzed their own process for the casing model they used. Their analysis included:

- Lead time from mill to base

- Cycle time of stock

- Price per delivered ton of casings

- Logistic costs divided into elements

- Inspection costs per ton

Because of time constraints, a desire to save money and the fact that this was their first project, they decided to benchmark against other companies within the industry. They identified four oil and gas companies in the North Sea to be their benchmarking partners and sent them questionnaires as a way to gather information about what each did.

Sample questions included:

What proportion of materials and services are supplied by vendors?

What is the number of variants in your casing assortment?

What is the hours per year required for the administration of the casing storage?

What costs are added at the different links of the supply chain?

By comparing and contrasting their casing with their partners' models, Statoil discovered they were using the most expensive casing model. By taking the best from each of the other models studied, they were able to make improvements that they estimate conservatively save them $7.5 million U.S. dollars annually.

BENCHMARKING IN EUROPE (continued)

An Historical Example

Quality expert Joseph M. Juran was quoted in the January 1994 issue of *Management Review* about the importance of benchmarking: "I think benchmarking—trying to discover what's the best performance around—is a useful idea relative to not having something suddenly come out of nowhere and hit us." Juran described an historical example of benchmarking: how the German military learned how to do it better from a most unlikely place.

CASE STUDY: A Creative Solution

Early in the century, some German generals undertook to follow an American circus. In those days, circuses didn't perform in huge arenas; they performed under tents, which are huge things to set up and take apart. Of course, circuses moved from city to city, and in some cases, they moved in a few hours. Workers would take everything down, put it on a train and take it to the next town. Striking a circus is very complicated. Animals and people must be fed and moved, gear must be packed and stored safely. In fact, special railway cars were designed to enable all this to happen, and circus workers were very good at it.

The generals had the same problem. They had all kinds of people. They had horses, ammunition, food—and they learned about deployment from seeing an operation that had no relation to an army.

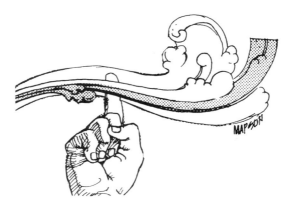

Benchmarking confirms the belief that there is a need for change.
—Robert C. Camp

S E C T I O N

II

Why Benchmarking?

WHAT ARE THE BENEFITS TO BENCHMARKING?

You do not have to do this, survival is not compulsory.
—W. Edwards Deming

Benchmarking ideally will create constant improvement and change within your organization. More and more organizations, in both manufacturing and service, are finding that adapting from the best can revitalize every facet of their operations. Benchmarking can be used to identify areas in which you can make significant improvements by adapting or matching systems that are proven better.

You can improve 12 areas of organizational activity by using benchmarking.

#1. Meeting Customer Requirements

By examining other organizations' successful processes, you often can get valuable information on consumer demand and responses within your industry. Adapting the best practices of others, wherever they are, will help you meet and beat customer expectations—the best way to match and surpass your competition. Best practices wouldn't exist if users didn't prefer them, and the best way to find out what customers want and whether you're meeting those requirements is to ask them. You'll find that the very best organizations consistently survey their customers.

In the past two years we have surveyed our customers for their opinions about

_____

_____

With the information we got from our customers, we _____

_____

_____

WHAT ARE THE BENEFITS TO BENCHMARKING? (continued)

#2. Adapting Industry-Best Practices

Benchmarking done right (making sure that a cross section of workers and managers directly participates in benchmarking teams) will ensure consensus support and enthusiasm for changes suggested by any benchmarking study.

#3. Becoming More Competitive

Benchmarking studies challenge long-held ideas by showing gaps between your organization's perceived performance and its actual competitive performance. Leading manufacturers develop new products up to two-and-a-half times faster than the industry average and for half the cost. The benchmarking gap is the difference between the industry average and the industry best.

Best-in-class error rates range from 500 to 1,000 times below industry averages. If you're average, these figures will be shocking. Those who get through the initial shock usually end up becoming much more competitive.

► Mortgage bankers compare their interest rates, service fees and product types weekly.

► *Financial World* rates the financial performance and management of major U.S. cities on a regular basis.

► JD Powers and Associates benchmarks customer-satisfaction levels among automobile owners.

Benchmarking against the competitive best also saves time and costs associated with the old way of improving: trial and error.

Our organization's error rate is _____,

which is ☐ above ☐ the same as ☐ below our industry's average.

We have verified this by _____.

#4. Setting Relevant, Realistic and Achievable Goals

Effective benchmarkers feel confident that their goals are realistic because they can link well-defined customer requirements with proven business practices. The major problems of blue-chip companies over the last few years can teach us an important lesson: Market forces can be quick and deadly and can destroy or hobble the strongest of organizations. Benchmarking helps organizations anticipate market changes and validate goals.

List three goals you would like to accomplish that will be more quickly attained by benchmarking.

1. _____

2. _____

3. _____

#5. Developing Accurate Measures of Productivity

By comparing your internal processes to best practices, leaders and employees get a better understanding of your company's strengths and weaknesses.

#6. Creating Support and Momentum for Internal Cultural Change

Benchmarking can sensitize your employees to the need for continual improvement in areas such as productivity growth, defect rate reduction and control of direct and indirect costs.

WHAT ARE THE BENEFITS TO BENCHMARKING? (continued)

#7. Setting and Refining Strategies

Strategic lessons learned earlier by other companies you choose to analyze can help your organization refine strategy, predict results of possible changes, and forecast changes in your market. With benchmarking, contingency plans can be developed and implemented faster and cheaper than if developed from scratch.

Bath Ironworks, the fourth largest shipyard in the United States and the largest employer in Maine, benchmarked the strategies and operations of 10 shipyards in The Netherlands when the end of the Cold War made the shipyard's business strategy out of date. Bath had just assumed the nation's need for combat ships would be strong for the rest of the century.

To adjust to the changing environment, Bath looked at the strategy of Dutch shipyards, which had changed their strategy to build more merchant ships.

How is strategy developed in your company?

_____

_____

How have your company's strategies changed in the past two years?

_____

_____

#8. Warning of Failure

A benchmarking program should tell you if and when you start falling behind your competitors in cost, customer satisfaction, technology or business processes. Benchmarking can be a source of creative ideas for correcting or eliminating problems of a key business function.

#9. Testing the Effectiveness of Your Quality Program

Benchmarking will test whether your quality initiatives and your competitive strategy are sound.

#10. Reengineering

Benchmarking is a necessity for organizations engineering or reengineering their processes and systems. Experts say reengineering without benchmarking will produce flat 5%–10% improvements, not the 50%–75% performance improvements often seen with radical redesign like reengineering.

What products or services does your organization provide?

_____

_____

What tells you your products meet or exceed customer expectations?

_____

_____

What tells you your products or services are improving?

_____

_____

WHAT ARE THE BENEFITS TO BENCHMARKING? (continued)

#11. Promoting Better Problem Solving

Does benchmarking improve problem-solving ability, or is problem-solving ability necessary to benchmark? Probably both. Standard problem solving provides a framework that makes work teams more effective. Standard problem solving also prompts teams to root their analysis in empirical data, which supports management-by-fact, a key ingredient in developing and maintaining a quality organization.

#12. Providing an Education and Creativity Boost

People become used to operating in certain ways. Even if those ways are harmful, most people resist changing because the old way of doing business is so comfortable. What benchmarking does is challenge the old way.

Regular benchmarking is like cleaning out your closet. You always find some things you don't need and a few things you didn't know you had, but could use. Regular benchmarking of critical functions ensures that you and your managers and employees remain open to new ideas, evolving technologies and changing trends.

Your organization encourages learning, creativity and teamwork by

_____

_____

What is your perception of your organization's commitment to learning?

_____

_____

OBJECTIONS TO BENCHMARKING

Benchmarking makes sense, but many organizations and leaders discourage the borrowing of others' good ideas. For example, many executives spend too much time on "problem" units or individuals. A benchmarking pro would instead spend more time with top-performing units or individuals and try to understand why they are so outstanding.

Some see benchmarking as cheating or industrial espionage. The fast-learning, big-achieving companies have a "we can learn from anyone" attitude that encourages the sharing of non-proprietary ideas and systems.

Others say benchmarking is nothing but copycatting, a system that leaves no room for improvement, but the most successful benchmarkers know that you don't adopt, you *adapt* processes and systems to your unique business. Edison may get credit for the light bulb, but it was the research of the nameless who came before him that Edison used in his experiments. Still others are afraid to benchmark because they don't want to expose their weaknesses to other world-class standards.

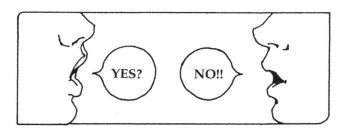

Should You Benchmark?

Ask the following questions to see if you should benchmark.

1. Can Your Organization Afford to Stop Improving?

2. Can Your Organization Afford to Stop Learning?

3. Can Your Organization Afford to Stop Competing for Its Position in the Marketplace?

If you answered no to any of these questions, you should benchmark.

OBJECTIONS TO BENCHMARKING
(continued)

Convincing Your Boss

By now you should have a good idea of what benchmarking is, who has benchmarked and what the benefits and criticisms of benchmarking are. Let's see if you can convince your boss of the need to benchmark.

Most of us try to convince others to do something by stressing why it is important to us. That is a major mistake. Your boss wants to know why he or she should benchmark. What is in it for the company?

 Write a clear, concise, to-the-point statement of the problem. The attitude of most people you try to persuade will be, "What do you want me to do? Why should I do it?" Make sure the problem statement you come up with is a problem for your persuasive target, his or her unit or the company. Be brief.

Write your problem statement here.

_____

_____

 Describe for your target the specimc, tangible, negative effects the problem has on him or her. How much does the problem cost in money, time, production or quality? You have to know your target well to be able to pinpoint the most effective negative effects to use. Use more than one in your argument: where one may not sell, a second or third may.

Brainstorm a list of five negative, tangible effects the problem has on your target. Don't be afraid to get suggestions from others. Then use no more than the top three.

1. _____

2. _____

3. _____

4. _____

5. _____

 **STEP 3** Describe your solutions to the problem. Offer more than one alternative for a target who may need convincing or is hostile to your proposition. People like to be presented with alternatives, but sometimes one solution is enough.

Write down three solutions to the problem.

1. _____

2. _____

3. _____

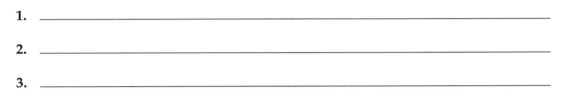 **STEP 4** Describe all the specific, tangible positive results that will come to your target, his or her unit, or the company by using your solution. How much money or time is saved? How much will quality improve? How much market share will the company gain?

Brainstorm a list of five positive, tangible effects the solution will have on your target. Don't be afraid to get suggestions from others. Then use no more than the top three.

1. _____

2. _____

3. _____

4. _____

5. _____

Now you have a structure for a logical argument to persuade anybody in your organization that your company needs to benchmark. Use this structure, write out your argument (do not think you can keep it in your head) and practice! This exercise won't guarantee 100% success in persuading others, but it will get you a lot closer than trying to persuade others based on what you want.

Like rowing upstream, not to advance is to drop back.
— Chinese proverb

Types of Benchmarking

SIX TYPES OF BENCHMARKING

You must continuously compare yourself against the very best.
In this game, good enough seldom is.
—Richard Dolinsky

Benchmarking started in the industrial sector, but it has now expanded into service, financial and government agencies. The Internal Revenue Service has benchmarked against American Express on billing and Motorola for accounting practices. Benchmarking is starting to show up in education, too.

Six distinct kinds of benchmarking seem to be emerging. The method best for you will be based on the kind and size of your organization and the purpose of the benchmark.

Internal Benchmarking

This ought to be the first type of benchmarking anybody does. First, know yourself. Know your internal processes. Look within units and across units or divisions to benchmark.

This kind of benchmarking is the fastest and cheapest to do. You can usually benchmark internal processes in less than six months. It is best to use internal benchmarking to assist processes that are critical to your unit's operations and those that have been changed by other managers in other units.

Internal benchmarking is the easiest of the six to manage, since both sides of the benchmark work for the same company. It is the least threatening kind of benchmark for management, which makes it the easiest of the six to sell to leaders. However, it can be the most difficult kind of benchmark to sell if the units being benchmarked are in an internally competitive environment.

Internal benchmarking ensures the easiest management of idea exchange and availability of partners, since all the information is under the same roof (or company). The information gathered is most easily used, since all parties should be using the same measurement system and speaking the same language.

Internal benchmarking has the lowest risk of failure in adapting the information to the organization, but internal benchmarking has the lowest benefit level, since you are simply looking at your own processes. The key benefit here is to look at your own internal processes and work harder and smarter to improve.

SIX TYPES OF BENCHMARKING (continued)

Competitive Benchmarking

Your organization probably is reluctant to share trade secrets with direct competitors, and this makes competitive benchmarking one of the most difficult kinds of benchmarking. Competitive benchmarking involves specific competitor-to-competitor comparisons, typically of a key product or process. One of the problems with this type of analysis is that some organizations participating in a competitive benchmark may purposely try to mislead the benchmarker by providing false data.

Many companies do participate with competitors for mutual benefits. For example, many of the major automotive companies benchmark each other on plant tours. You don't typically exchange information; you exchange plant visits and you have to pick it up on your own.

Not all competitors are cooperative, but if you can get to enough plants and gather enough information through public records, magazine articles, your own sales force and suppliers, you may get close to what you need. However you collect data on competitors, the goal is to find out what the competition is doing and how your processes compare with theirs.

On average, competitive benchmarking is faster and cheaper (six to twelve months) than all other methods except internal benchmarking because you compare processes you share with competitors. This type of benchmarking is difficult to manage if your competitors are uncooperative. In that case, you must depend more on indirect data, which is less valuable than direct competitive comparisons.

Keep in mind that 90% of all information you need to make key decisions and to understand your market and competitors is already public or can be developed from public data. In gathering competitive intelligence, your sources can include:

- Department of Commerce
- Literature searches
- Newspapers and magazines
- Associations
- Competitor's press releases
- Plant tours
- Released legal documents
- Interviews
- Clearinghouses
- Databases
- Internet
- Questionnaires

Competitive benchmarking projects are harder to sell to managers because they may fear they will be giving information away to competitors. However, it can be easier to use competitive benchmark data because the information comes from the same industry, and you might even employ people who have worked for these competitors.

The risks in using the information you gather from a competitive benchmark are moderate since you're gathering data from competitors within your industry.

In approaching direct competitors, the questionnaire/interview method may not give you much useful information. They might feel threatened by the possibility that the information they offer might give you a competitive advantage you don't already have.

While this approach might not work, it is certainly worth trying. In fact, in some industries, the direct approach is the best way.

For the direct approach to work, one of the following factors must be present:

► A history of strategic alliances among companies in the industry, which already includes some data exchange

► The targeted company does not perceive itself as a direct competitor

► Nonthreatening data is sought, such as the way employee suggestions are handled

Do not count on the direct approach to provide all the information and details you need. It is more realistic to combine any information competitors give you with information you have gathered from your public domain data-gathering.

The benefit you get from competitive benchmarking is a chance to learn how to do something better from an outside perspective. The results are also better than what you would get from benchmarking only against yourself, and it is easier to transfer information you get on competitors' processes to your own organization. However, if you only *copy* the competition instead of *adapting* the information to fit your needs, *you will only be as good as your competitor, not better.*

SIX TYPES OF BENCHMARKING (continued)

Convincing Your Competitor

Let's see if you can design an argument to convince a competitor to allow you to benchmark against one of their processes. Remember, you need to convince them what is in it for them.

 Write a clear, concise statement about what information you are interested in gathering from your target. Keep your request as nonthreatening as possible.

_____

_____

 Describe specific, tangible benefits *they* will get from allowing you to benchmark. Brainstorm with others if you need to. Choose the top three reasons.

1. _____

2. _____

3. _____

(Collaborative Benchmarking)

An alternative to competitive benchmarking, collaborative benchmarking involves a limited exchange of information from a consortium of (sometimes anonymous) companies. This may be a good way for organizations to get started, since collaborative benchmarking is cheaper than competitive benchmarking and typically takes far less time than six to twelve months. Your industry's professional organizations may have or be willing to start a "best practices" collaborative benchmarking database. Other ad-hoc groups can be formed and managed by outside consultants.

Collaborative benchmarking usually focuses only on quantitative statistics rather than qualitative analysis. Although this approach has limited usefulness, in conjunction with other benchmarking methods you may get worthwhile ideas.

Shadow Benchmarking

Making competitor-to-competitor comparisons without your benchmarking partner knowing you're doing it is called shadow benchmarking. Normally more expensive than competitive benchmarking, shadow benchmarking takes six to twelve months to complete.

The types of processes that are best improved by shadowing are those that you have in common with the partner; the quality and relevance of the collected data depends on how specific management is in targeting the shadow partner and how experienced the benchmarking team is in data gathering and analysis. Shadowing is much easier to sell to management if it is related to increased market penetration or when management is highly competitive.

Shadowing entails no real partner so you aren't dependent on competitor cooperation, and information comes from whatever competitive intelligence you can gather. Some ideas may be harder to transfer directly to your organization, but the information can be useful in preventing investment errors and in redirecting resources to meet competitive challenges.

Risks in adapting the information to your organization are somewhat higher because you may have incomplete data, but shadow benchmarking lets you gather new data that will help you improve your processes or prepare yourself for market growth without alerting competitors.

Functional Benchmarking

This kind of benchmarking compares your processes with similar, but not identical, processes within the same industry, often with industry leaders.

Functional benchmarking takes more time. Your first functional or industrial benchmark normally lasts 12–15 months.

The processes best helped with industrial benchmarking are those that look to the future. This analysis seeks new ideas that have already succeeded in a compatible area. However, managing this effort gets more difficult as the number of targets and processes increases.

It's harder to sell this form of benchmarking to leaders because it takes more time and preparation than other benchmarking forms. The potential number of partners is much greater, but because they aren't in direct competition, they may be more willing to cooperate in data exchanges. Because many of the partners are from different cultures and industries, the information is harder to transfer to your organization.

SIX TYPES OF BENCHMARKING (continued)

The risks in adapting the information you gather can be high, since you're making changes for the future direction of your organization, yet are manageable, since you control collection and analysis of benchmarking data. The benefits can also be high, because you are making changes based on the operations of organizations that are not your direct competitors—which might allow you to surpass your competitors.

World-Class Benchmarking

Comparing processes that are the same regardless of industry (including order entry, marketing and telephone sales) with world-class organizations that are outside of your industry establishes you in world-class benchmarking. This kind of benchmarking:

✔ Takes the longest time to prepare and execute. Budget 12–24 months to carry out your first project and apply the findings.

✔ Can be difficult to manage because the most easily identified partners are often reluctant to participate. They are inundated with requests that take time and money, and you have to prove to them that they will get something from the exchange. A cheaper and less time-consuming alternative is to look for benchmarking partners that are near world-class. Information from this kind of benchmark is the hardest to transfer to your organization, since data often comes from very different kinds of companies.

✔ Is hard to sell to leaders because of the greater time and money required. Moreover, risks in adapting the information are high, since the data gathered often suggests fundamental changes in leadership and operations. Risks can be controlled by doing this kind of benchmarking after you have done the others first.

The benefits can be the greatest in world-class benchmarking, however, because you may get ideas that improve your key processes tremendously.

DECIDING WHAT KIND IS BEST FOR YOU

You can't really say that one form of benchmarking is better than another; however, one might be more appropriate for your organization depending on your environment, product or service and your stage of organizational development.

Always begin with the reason you exist: your customers. Once you start to benchmark, you will find that the best companies all have a passion for communicating with their internal and external customers. Regular mail and telephone surveys, focus groups, person-to-person interviews, and informal customer contacts will help you discover how you're doing and what your customer really wants and needs of you. In addition to letting you respond more quickly to customer wants and problems, contact will also send an important message to your customers that you care. Can you think of any examples when you as a customer were frustrated with a supplier? Chances are great it had to do with their failure to communicate with you. Have you ever been angry at an airline for a late departure? Was your anger intensified because nobody kept you informed? Most customers can handle bad news better if the organization just communicates with us.

Internal Benchmarking

This acts as a good training ground for your organization and should be your first step. You must understand your own processes before you can benchmark against others, and a good starting place in measuring your own processes is to compare your practices with those of the Malcolm Baldrige National Quality Award. Use the Baldrige Award criteria to benchmark internally your own company against those seven categories (see Appendix). Then benchmark your organization against your competitors.

Competitive Benchmarking

This is good for organizations that have some experience in benchmarking. It also works well when your industry has several competitors with many kinds of management philosophies and operating histories.

Collaborative Benchmarking

This may be right for you if all you want to do is compare statistics with other firms. This kind of benchmarking will not reveal qualitative results, but it can be useful if you use it in conjunction with other benchmarking methods. It might also suggest new ideas or indicate trends.

DECIDING WHAT KIND IS BEST FOR YOU (continued)

Shadow Benchmarking

This is best if you're trying to penetrate a new market that has strong competitors. It also works in a market where dominance in a process or technology can give a big advantage.

Functional Benchmarking

This is best if your organization has already done benchmarking, and you can see areas of expertise you can share with any potential partners. Larger firms tend to benefit more from this form of benchmarking because they have the resources to spend on the exercise.

World-Class Benchmarking

This is best for organizations that have significant experience in benchmarking and know how to apply what they've learned to improve their own processes.

Applying Benchmarking

PHASE 1: ⟶ Start with an internal "best practices" benchmarking program.

PHASE 2: ⟶ Continue with a competitive benchmark.

PHASE 3: ⟶ Follow up with a functional benchmark to see what best practices are outside your industry.

Based on your experience with benchmarking, your competitive position and your organization:

What kind of benchmarking is best for you?

_____

Why?

_____

Name three processes you know you want to benchmark.

1. _____

_____

2. _____

_____

3. _____

_____

GOING IT ALONE OR USING A CONSULTANT

If you're new to benchmarking, you're probably wondering whether you should do it yourself or hire a consultant. If you do hire a consultant, make sure you understand how he or she does it.

The benefits of doing it yourself include getting first-hand data. You just don't get that by reading a report. It takes more time to do it yourself, but you can get more information because it isn't distilled. The process can even be fun! However, many do-it-yourselfers have trouble arranging meetings and contacts and finding world-class or industry-specific leaders in the processes they're trying to benchmark.

The advantages of using a consultant are mainly educational. While experts claim experience, anybody can benchmark.

Consultants are best at data collection and analysis, a time-consuming process that many organizations can't afford. Consultants also save you time by wading through tons of irrelevant data, and they often have many contacts that can save time, too. If you decide to use a benchmarking consultant:

► Make sure they know what they're doing. Have them explain the benchmarking process to your satisfaction.

► Ask them to describe their benchmarking approach. Make sure it fits your organizational culture. Can you trust the abilities of this benchmarking consultant?

► Demand that they teach you what they do and how they do it. Make sure that is part of the agreement.

Should you benchmark yourself or work with a consultant?

_____

Why?

_____

BENCHMARKING FOR INDIVIDUALS

Most people assume that benchmarking is a search for best in-house or external organizational practices, but you can also adapt the benchmarking process to improve individual performance. Management and employees need to benchmark regularly how much their counterparts inside and outside the organization know and the rate they are learning. If you find out that others are learning faster than you, you need to find a way to match and pass them.

Use the benchmarking process to identify and learn from your top performers. Too many organizations focus too closely on intermediate to low performers—Numerous counseling sessions, training, cajoling—anything to bring up performance.

How much time does your organization spend learning from the top performers? Instead of asking "What are our low performers doing wrong?" ask "What are our top performers doing right?" If your organization is typical, you probably reward your top people at the yearly banquet and then forget about them the rest of the time.

Important Questions to Ask

Spend some time studying your high performers and answer the following questions. Regularly share this information with everybody in the organization. Ask these top performers:

Why are they that way?

_____

_____

_____

What do they do differently?

_____

_____

_____

BENCHMARKING FOR INDIVIDUALS
(continued)

What specific approaches and practices do they use?

_____

_____

_____

How can you leverage this intellectual capital in your organization to help others improve?

_____

_____

_____

If you could raise everybody to the level of top performers, how would that affect your bottom line?

_____

_____

_____

How would it improve quality?

_____

_____

_____

A good way to benchmark yourself externally is to participate in professional associations. You will find addresses and phone numbers in the *National Trade and Professional Associations Directory*, which can be found in any library's reference section. There are associations for every interest, trade and profession.

1. Name three individuals against whom you can benchmark.

- _____

- _____

- _____

2. What three specific individual performance or learning measures would you benchmark?

- _____

- _____

- _____

3. How can individual benchmarking help your employees, coworkers or leaders?

_____

_____

_____

BENCHMARKING FOR SERVICE ORGANIZATIONS

Even though benchmarking had its start in industry, you can still get a lot out of benchmarking if you work for a service organization. Industrial processes such as scheduling and distribution also are key processes in service organizations.

One service organization that benchmarks is an association called the Healthcare Forum of San Francisco. This association is made up of medical professionals and administrators in all 50 states. One way the association helps its membership is through four Quality Improvement Networks, each made up of 15 or more member organizations that share a commitment to quality improvement.

In the early 1990s, the Quality Improvement Networks decided to examine hospital admissions. Members knew that this first point of contact with a hospital was often difficult and confusing for patients. Moreover, hospital staff also found it confusing. Some patients are referred by doctors; others, who come in through emergency rooms, have no referring doctors. For routine admissions, the staff must find out whether tests already have been performed or whether they should be performed. Then they must arrange for payment and get the patient a room.

When these benchmarking members began looking for benchmarking partners, they looked at other kinds of businesses that handled similar processes. Hotels had to register guests and arrange for payment. Airlines had to book space and arrange schedules and payment. Eventually, members decided to focus on their own industry. They arranged to benchmark against 28 hospitals.

The members realized that studying admitting processes was too broad. They would have to refine their study into admission practices for inpatients, out-patients and emergency patients. They decided to focus on the admissions of elective, acute-care patients. Then they developed a plan for the study and mailed a questionnaire to the 28 participating hospitals to:

► Identify best-practice candidates (looking for the most quantifiably efficient hospitals committed to quality improvement)

► Measure the admitting process (collecting data on the efficiency and economy of the admitting process of each of the 28 hospitals)

When the questionnaires were returned, members identified the five or six best hospitals based on waiting times of less than five minutes and accuracy of patient information greater than 95%. The group members rated each hospital's "opportunity for improvement" in customer satisfaction, information technology and measurement techniques. The members then were able to identify key areas that could help the hospitals improve their admitting processes. This included training admitting staff adequately using modern information technology and reducing the number of admitting forms.

Great discoveries and improvements invariably involve
the cooperation of many minds.

—Alexander Graham Bell

S E C T I O N

IV

Ready, Set, Go!

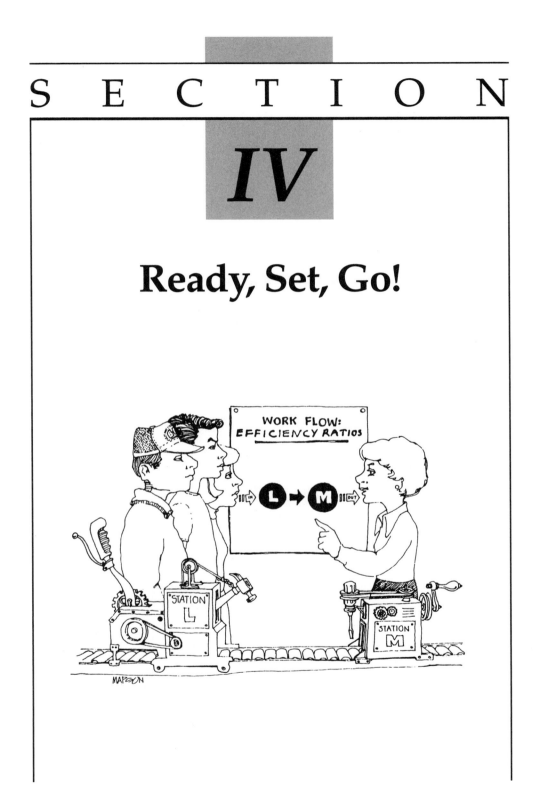

BEFORE YOU START TO BENCHMARK

When you aim for perfection, you discover it is a moving target.
—George Fisher

Benchmarking can produce measurable quality results for your organization, but it is no quick fix. A good benchmarking study needs time, labor, money and planning, and benchmarking is a continuous process. So what does your organization need before you can begin benchmarking?

▶ **Absolute and total leadership commitment.**

Make sure management doesn't offer just token support; they must show employees how important benchmarking is by actively participating in it. Benchmarking can require considerable organizational resources and it affects organizational goals. If you do not have complete leadership commitment to your benchmarking project, do not benchmark. You will fail and management will blame you.

▶ **Being open to change and other, different ideas.**

For benchmarking to work and thrive, you and other employees and managers must accept that improving and competing mean being open to new ideas and willing to adapt ideas wherever you find them.

▶ **Truly knowing your own organization's operations.**

Part of the definition of benchmarking is comparing your operation's processes against other processes. To adapt what you learn from a benchmarking study, you must first know your own processes.

▶ **Being willing to share the results of your benchmarking study with your benchmarking partners.**

You need not share trade secrets, but you must give information about your processes in an effort to get theirs. Remember, the best companies didn't get that way by looking only inward.

▶ **A leadership dedicated to continuous quality improvement through benchmarking.**

Leaders must show they are committed to quality through a continuous process of benchmarking improvement.

BEFORE YOU START TO BENCHMARK (continued)

Are You Ready to Benchmark?

Place a checkmark by the statement that reflects where your organization is today.

☐ STAGE 1: INSPECTION

Inspection is the earliest stage of quality in your organization. If you're at this stage, make sure you have high quality through productive inspections. Employees will inspect by measurements, standards, calibration and testing.

If this looks like your company, don't start a benchmarking program yet. To get the full benefits of benchmarking, everybody in your organization should learn how to use the basic quality skills like interpersonal communication, problem solving and decision making. Then people ought to be encouraged to use and better those skills.

☐ STAGE 2: CONTROL

Control is the second stage of quality. Here, everybody in the organization uses their skills to prevent most quality problems from happening in the first place. Your organization also uses inspection and more sophisticated techniques such as statistical process control and teamwork.

☐ STAGE 3: PARTNERSHIP

Partnership is the third stage of quality in an organization. You know you're here when leaders and employees work together to meet shared goals that have been clearly communicated to everybody in the organization. People don't see themselves as isolated individuals of the organization; they identify themselves as members of the team.

Organizations at this third stage will benefit the most from a benchmarking program.

What You Should Benchmark

If you're doing it, you can benchmark it. You should benchmark what is important to your business and what you know can be improved, but you may not know what you can improve and what is important until you're doing your first benchmarking effort. There are seven guidelines for selecting the best functions, processes or products you should benchmark.

1. **Those that make up the highest percentage of fixed or variable costs**
2. **Anything that affects quality, costs or cycle times**
3. **Processes or functions of most strategic importance to your organization**
4. **Anything you do that has the greatest room for improvement**
5. **Whatever you do that you can improve**
6. **Anything that supports the company's or your department's success**
7. **Any factors that separate your organization from the competition**

Business Process Rankings

The top business processes (out of a total of 110 processes) *The Benchmarking Exchange* members are benchmarking.*

BUSINESS PROCESS	RANKING: 1991 to 1994	1993 ONLY	1994 ONLY
Information Systems	1	1	5
Human Resources	2	42	1
Training	3	2	11
Compensation	4	6	2
Benchmarking	5	5	16
Quality	6	10	3
Finance	7	31	6
Supplier Management	8	11	4
Customer Service	9	3	15
Product Development	10	4	13

*Information provided by Tom Dolan, *The Benchmarking Exchange*, Aptos, California.

BEFORE YOU START TO BENCHMARK
(continued)

Benchmarking Trends

Information Systems

This is ranked the number one process to benchmark over the past four years but was fifth in 1994. Why? Organizations have been able to move on to other business processes that require attention. Companies have recognized that without an information systems infrastructure, managing other business processes would be very difficult, if not impossible.

Compensation and Human Resources

These have received more attention in 1994 compared with recent years. Both processes can affect one another and very commonly in the same direction. Consider that more than 50% of Fortune 500 organizations have had layoffs within the past two years. To quote *Fortune,* "Every year since 1988, at least one-third of large and midsize U.S. companies have pared their workforces." Experts say to look for these two business processes to remain high on the benchmarking list throughout the next year.

Benchmarking the Benchmarking Process

This has also received a lot of attention. One of the best ways to get started in benchmarking is by studying those who have already done it. Now that many organizations know benchmarking, a move to practice what they have learned is taking shape.

Quality

This is another process high on the benchmarking charts. For years, leaders thought they were doing their part in the practice of quality. They did it all and still couldn't understand why their efforts didn't pay off. Something was missing. Now, companies are refocusing attention on their quality management process by benchmarking the process itself.

LEARNING TO BENCHMARK: THE *PDCA* CYCLE

Benchmarking is a cycle of continuous improvement. The best way to understand the process is through the *PDCA* (Plan, Do, Check, Act) *Cycle*.

P Any quality improvement process starts with the **P**, or *Plan*. The plan can be a large-scale organizational review of operations or a small-scale unit plan to learn how best to carry out a simple task. No matter how big the process is, it should be subject of constant scrutiny. Planning shouldn't be seen only as something you do before you start a new process; you should also do it as a means of constant evaluation.

A plan is anything that might improve a process, whether it happens at the point the process begins or at any other later point. If you can't tie any planned change to your organization's mission (satisfying customer needs), don't consider it.

You should also have a way to evaluate the effectiveness of the plan. How will you know the plan has been successful if you can't measure its progress?

D Now that you have a customer-oriented plan, you're ready to put it into action. At first, test the plan on a limited scale. This is the **D** or *Do* phase. By limiting the scope of the project, you can minimize the cost or time that might be wasted on an unsuccessful change. Now is the time to gather data related to the plan.

C The **C** or *Check* phase of the cycle entails examining the data to discover if the plan and implemented change has created the quality improvement you intended.

A In the **A**, or *Act* phase, your data may suggest that you run through a second PDCA cycle to change the variables to see if you can improve the process, or you might decide to standardize the process as it is.

Then the next step is back to the Plan, where you again try to improve your operations in the full cycle of continuous improvement.

LEARNING TO BENCHMARK: THE *PDCA* CYCLE (continued)

Before you conduct a full-scale benchmarking study, make sure to follow these three steps:

STEP 1: Identify the areas you want to improve and the goals you want to achieve that will satisfy and exceed customer requirements. Concentrate first on the most important areas.

STEP 2: Understand the processes you plan to study.

STEP 3: Focus on the underlying practices and processes you use to achieve better results in the areas you want to improve.

BENCHMARKING WITH THE PDCA CYCLE

No one best step-by-step procedure will ensure benchmarking success. However, there are a number of good models. The one thing all the models have in common is that they all follow the PDCA cycle.

PHASE 1: Plan

#1. Make sure all your employees know what benchmarking is, believe in its benefits and feel empowered to do the study and implement findings. Many organizations agree that the best way to get people involved in benchmarking is by first doing a small internal benchmarking study without a lot of training. Eight to sixteen hours of training should be enough. The first hands-on project will be the best kind of training. Afterward, make sure all the benchmarkers evaluate their work to assess successes, errors and areas for improvement.

#2. Make sure management is committed to benchmarking, because they will have to commit time, allocate resources, remove roadblocks and reward the effort. Time is probably the biggest issue because most benchmarking studies will take at least six months to complete. A great way to show leadership commitment to benchmarking is to involve management in the benchmarking team's training and activities, but any benchmarking or quality effort that begins without leadership support and participation will fail.

#3. What should you benchmark? Start with the customer. Customers will tell you when you make mistakes. Measure and track customer reactions. Collect data, good or bad, through formal surveys (telephone, mail, in-person interviews), and internal and external sales people. You can discover benchmarking opportunities by asking two questions: "Has anyone ever faced a similar problem before? What did they do about it?" Use the criteria in this checklist to decide if a topic is right for your benchmarking study.

❑ *Is the topic important to our customers?*

❑ *Is the topic consistent with our mission, values and milestones?*

❑ *Does the topic reflect an important business need?*

❑ *Is the topic significant in terms of costs or key nonfinancial indicators?*

❑ *Is the topic in an area where additional information could influence plans and actions?*

Topics for benchmarking studies can include any process that is vital for customer satisfaction and company success.

BENCHMARKING WITH THE PDCA CYCLE (continued)

#4. Now you need to create a benchmarking project action plan. Successful benchmarking organizations make sure that they cover the following areas:

- **Goals and Objectives**
- **Scope and Resources**
- **Key Players**
- **Critical Success Factors**

- **Roles and Responsibilities**
- **Milestones and Deliverables**
- **Performance Measures**
- **High-Level Process Flows**

The benchmarking team should choose a leader, a benchmarking and meeting process guide, recorder and timekeeper. Then the team needs to decide the purpose of their study.

Here are some good questions the team needs to answer.

Who are the customers for the study? _____

_____

What is the scope of the study? _____

_____

What characteristics will we measure? _____

_____

What information about the topic can we easily get? _____

_____

Brainstorm to determine that the problem exists. If it does, the team should use problem-solving tools* to develop the proposal.

---

*For more information on this topic order *Facilitation Skills for Team Leaders* by Donald Hackett and Charles Martin. Crisp Publications. 1993.

Once you select a process to benchmark, you need to study how you perform the process. You won't be able to ask intelligent questions about other people's processes if you don't understand your own. You also need to benchmark your process so you can have data of value to share with any partner. Benchmarking without fully understanding your own processes guarantees failure. One of your team's biggest challenges will be to match your process measurements to that of another organization. You can normally accomplish this by asking your benchmarking partner, "Here's what we're looking for . . . how do you measure it here?"

#5. Once you and your team have written the benchmarking plan and it is approved, you need to select benchmarking partners. Here's another opportunity for your team to practice brainstorming. Generate two dozen organizations you could benchmark against, using:

- Suppliers
- Trade Magazines
- Internal and External Customers
- Your Professional Associations
- Your Customers' Associations
- Trade Shows
- Industry Experts
- Industry Studies

From the original two dozen companies you have identified, narrow your field to six using the following criteria matrix. Experience shows you may get half to three-quarters of these organizations to agree to a benchmarking project.

USE THE FOLLOWING CRITERIA MATRIX

EXERCISE: *Benchmarking Partner Criteria Matrix*

Use the following chart to evaluate potential benchmarking partners. From your initial two dozen or so benchmarking prospects, select the top half-dozen companies for further evaluation based on the following criteria. Add or subtract from the criteria given according to what is important to your business, competitors, industry and customers (5 = Excellent, 1 = Poor).

Criteria Matrix

CRITERIA	Co. #1	Co. #2	Co. #3	Co. #4	Co. #5	Co. #6
1. *Quality orientation*						
2. *Service orientation*						
3. *High product or service reputation*						
4. *Excellent cycle time*						
5. *100% reliability*						
6. *Company size*						
7. *25% improvement in year-to-year sales growth*						
8. *25% improvement in year-to-year profitability*						
9. _____						
10. _____						
11. _____						
TOTALS =						

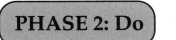

PHASE 2: Do

#6. This phase entails collecting benchmarking data with your partners. You need to agree on a time frame for the study and any site visit, an agenda and the questions you'll ask. Use the fax machine and telephone to speed up communication. Not all benchmarking has to include a site visit: Many organizations report excellent benchmarking results by relying on the fax, mail and telephone for data gathering with other organizations.

Once you make contact with an organization, ask the following questions and note the answers in the space provided.

Does the company have a defined, documented process? _____

_____

How is the process communicated to the process customers and users? _____

_____

_____

How are the users kept up to date on the process changes? _____

_____

_____

What is the management system of the process? _____

_____

_____

What aspects of the process are considered to be world-class? _____

_____

_____

BENCHMARKING WITH THE PDCA CYCLE (continued)

Your team can cover site visits in groups of two or three. Go in with a common set of questions to ask, make sure everybody records the answers, then compare your answers during lunch and dinner. Remember:

- **Never ask a question you wouldn't answer at your home organization.**

- **Never ask a question you wouldn't be able to answer about your own processes** (bring your home organization's process data with you for reference)

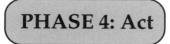

PHASE 3: Check

#7. The data you gather in benchmarking will serve many purposes. Quantifying performance will clarify your organization's processes. Then comparing your process to others' should identify performance gaps between what is and what could be. The larger the gap between you and the other organization, the greater the need for you to improve.

PHASE 4: Act

#8. Now you are ready to take your data and apply it to improve your organization's processes. To understand better what you have, you and your team should compare your partners' answers to each question you ask about a process. What do each of the partners you've benchmarked do about a certain process? What are the results?

Then select the process that seems to work the best, adapt it to your organization, try it for a test period and evaluate the results. If it works, implement the improvement. Make sure you measure and monitor the new process to see if it continues to perform as expected. Always strive to improve the new process. This is a continuous, never-ending job. Just follow the PDCA cycle for your next benchmarking project, and use PDCA to follow up on your current benchmarking project.

Make sure you and your team share benchmarking data with everybody in your organization. An excellent and efficient way to do this is through a company newsletter. Share your success and failures with all and ask for everybody's suggestions and help.

Not every benchmarking study will result in change. Sometimes the necessary changes cost too much or just won't work for you.

BENCHMARKING ACTION PLAN CHECKLIST

Use the following checklist to keep your benchmarking project on track. Be specific in describing how you accomplished each step or how you will accomplish each step.

PDCA Benchmarking Step-by-Step

PLAN

Yes	No	Partial	
☐	☐	☐	1. Have you established your benchmarking objectives?
☐	☐	☐	2. Have you informed, trained and involved employees?
☐	☐	☐	3. Do you have complete leadership commitment?
☐	☐	☐	4. Have you decided what to benchmark?
☐	☐	☐	5. Have you studied your own processes and do you understand them?

BENCHMARKING ACTION PLAN CHECKLIST (continued)

Yes	No	Partial	
☐	☐	☐	6. Have you created a benchmarking action plan?

_____
_____
_____

Yes	No	Partial	
☐	☐	☐	7. Have you chosen benchmarking partners?

_____
_____
_____

DO

Yes	No	Partial	
☐	☐	☐	8. Have you collected benchmarking data with your partners?

_____
_____
_____

CHECK

Yes	No	Partial	
☐	☐	☐	9. Have you analyzed the benchmarking data you collected?

_____
_____
_____

ACT

Yes	No	Partial	
☐	☐	☐	10. Have you adapted and applied the information you learned?

_____
_____
_____

(Repeat PDCA Cycle)

THE ETHICS OF BENCHMARKING

How do you make sure you and your partners gain and not lose from benchmarking? The International Benchmarking Clearinghouse (IBC) of the American Productivity and Quality Center has established a code of conduct for benchmarkers that includes many of the following.

► Obey the law. Don't do anything that might imply restraint of trade, bid rigging, price fixing or acquisition of trade secrets. If you agree to share proprietary information, make sure all parties sign a nondisclosure agreement.

► Be prepared from the start. Don't waste your benchmarking partners' time by learning on their time.

► Be willing to give partners the same kind of information you want. Make sure all partners know what to expect to avoid later misunderstandings. Don't assume anything.

► Respect confidentiality. Treat any information you gain from benchmarking as confidential unless you get your partner's written permission.

► Keep benchmarking information inside your organization to improve the operational processes of your organization. Don't use the data in your advertising or promotional efforts.

► Follow the chain of command. Don't first approach the business unit; seek permission from the senior management of the parent company.

► Unless given permission, don't share benchmarking partners' names with others.

► Be honest.

SOLUTIONS TO COMMON BENCHMARKING MISTAKES

The reason you benchmark is to learn from others so you can improve your own processes. However, you can also learn from other people's benchmarking mistakes. This will save time and money and reduce the frustration.

Mistake 1: Lack of Leadership

SOLUTION: Every benchmarking team needs a leader. And every team needs a sponsor, or top-level leader, who understands why you're benchmarking, what the goals are, how they relate to the organization's goals, the time-frame involved, and pledges to support your efforts. To keep top leadership support, your benchmarking team must keep leaders informed all along the way. If possible, try to include senior leaders directly in benchmarking projects.

Mistake 2: Picking the Wrong People for Your Benchmarking Team

SOLUTION: The best people for your benchmarking team are those directly involved in the process being studied. The people working directly with the process are your subject matter experts. And make sure you don't force participation. There is nobody worse for a benchmarking team than a person who doesn't want to be there. Select only motivated volunteers.

Mistake 3: Failing to Consider Strategic Long-Term Objectives

SOLUTION: Focus on processes related to the long-term strategy rather than short-term problems.

Mistake 4: Too Many People on the Team

SOLUTION: Some organizations have put as many as thirty people on a benchmarking team. This guarantees disaster. Communication among and between members will be impossible and some will do most of the work while others will do none. Six to eight on a team is ideal.

Mistake 5: Teams Taking on Too Much

SOLUTION: Sometimes teams take on topics so broad that the project is unmanageable. Be specific. Break down the project into manageable parts. For example, create a functional flowchart of an entire area such as production and identify its processes. Then select a process or processes to benchmark that would best contribute to your organization's objectives.

Mistake 6: Leadership Underestimates Time Commitments

SOLUTION: Leaders often are not as familiar with the day-to-day work issues of the organization as their employees are, so they may not understand the cost and time needed to fix a problem. Because of the pressures of competition, leaders often want quick solutions; some company leaders have allowed only four weeks for a benchmarking team to conduct a study. Remind leadership that benchmarking studies require at least six months.

Mistake 7: Picking the Wrong Benchmarking Partners

SOLUTION: Make sure you have something to give in return. This should be a free exchange of information. Both or all sides must win.

Mistake 8: Assuming Every Project Needs a Site Visit

SOLUTION: Sometimes you can accomplish much just through mail or telephone surveys and a literature search. Make sure you can justify a site visit.

Mistake 9: Management Failing to Inspect Benchmarking Results

SOLUTION: Management should follow the PDCA cycle in reviewing changes made in processes as a result of a benchmarking project.

SOLUTIONS TO COMMON BENCHMARKING MISTAKES (continued)

Mistake 10: Failing to Identify Targets in Advance

SOLUTION: Before you start to work with your benchmarking partners, understand how you will use any data collected. Refer to the action plan you have created.

Mistake 11: Collecting Too Much Data

SOLUTION: Don't get buried in a lot of useless data, hoping you will find a nugget or two of gold.

Mistake 12: Focusing on Numerical Targets Rather Than the Process

SOLUTION: Some organizations still focus their benchmarking efforts on performance targets (metrics) rather than processes. The problem with this focus is that even if the organization hits its performance target, it won't know how to do so again. Focusing on performance *gaps* can be useful in seeing improvement opportunities. Knowledge of those gaps can be motivating for a team to accelerate performance improvement in its area by mapping its process.

The damn thing won't fly at all until top management
people are 100 percent behind it. Where is the bottle-neck?
Just look at the top of the bottle and you will find it.

—Bill Conway

BENCHMARKING QUICK CHECK

How well do you understand benchmarking? Practice here before you approach senior management with a benchmarking project idea. Remember to follow the four step persuasive argument process.

1. What is benchmarking?

_____

_____

_____

2. Where did it start?

_____

_____

_____

3. What are the benefits of benchmarking?

_____

_____

_____

4. What are the arguments against benchmarking?

_____

_____

_____

BENCHMARKING QUICK CHECK

5. Describe two of the six kinds of benchmarking.

_____

_____

_____

6. What kind of benchmarking is best to start with? Why?

_____

_____

_____

7. What is the PDCA cycle? How does it relate to the eight steps of benchmarking?

_____

_____

_____

8. During your benchmarking project, how did you make sure you accomplished each of the eight steps?

_____

_____

_____

BENCHMARKING REVIEW

#1. Define your benchmarking objectives.

#2. Agree on a common way to measure processes.

#3. Understand your own processes before benchmarking against others, and remember that this will take more time than you think.

#4. Be open to the fact that others might be better than you.

#5. Assign one manager for the benchmarking process.

#6. Have a well-balanced relationship among the ambitions for the project, the time available, and the resources you are willing to invest.

#7. Avoid the industrial tourism trap.

#8. Remember that benchmarking is not just a fact-gathering process; you have to do something with your data.

#9. Put together a well-composed and trained project team.

#10. Identify and make arrangements with benchmarking partners early on, as it is a time-consuming process.

#11. Always keep your customers in mind.

#12. Follow up on what you learn.

IN CONCLUSION

Benchmarking is not simply a cookbook technique. Your organization is unique; it needs a specific recipe for your specific needs for your specific situation. Benchmarking is also not just collecting metrics, or numbers. How to achieve those numbers is the fundamental mission of benchmarking, but if all you do is collect numbers, all you'll accomplish is to be a good number collector. However, if you compare and contrast your process measurements with those organizations superior to yours, then you will learn to change for the better.

Benchmarking begins when you first learn what you do, then benchmark against yourself, decide (based heavily on customer needs) what processes to benchmark, and then determine whether you can take a cheaper, faster approach (such as library research) or go outside and benchmark processes with other competitors.

Benchmarking, like quality improvement, has no finish line. It is a continuous improvement process. You can improve the benchmarking process just as you can improve any process you do.

Just remember, if you aren't benchmarking now, you might want to reconsider. Your competitors are.

Total quality starts with and ends with training.
To implement total quality, we need to carry out
continuous education for everyone, from the
president down the line to the workers.

—Kaoru Ishikawa

S E C T I O N

V

Appendix

QUALITY AND BENCHMARKING REFERENCES

Publications

Altany, David. "Benchmarkers Unite." *Industry Week*, p. 25.

Bogan, Christopher E. and Michael J. English. "Benchmarking for Best Practices." *Quality Digest*, pp. 52–57.

Cortado, James W. and John A. Woods. *The Quality Yearbook: 1994 Edition.* New York: McGraw-Hill, 1994. (See "Steal this Idea," by Christopher Bogan and John Robbins, pp. 143–153; "Benchmarking: An Overview," by Calhoun W. Wick and LuStanton Leon, pp. 401–414; and "How to Build a Benchmarking Team," by Michael J. Spendolini, pp. 415–421)

Cortado, James W. and John A. Woods. *The Quality Yearbook: 1995 Edition.* New York: McGraw-Hill, 1995. (See "How to do Benchmarking," by James W. Cortado, pp. 733–737).

DeToro, Irving. "The 10 Pitfalls of Benchmarking." *Quality Progress*, January 1995, pp. 61–63.

Editors. *The Memory Joggers.* Methuen, MA: Goal/QPC, 1988.

George, Stephen and Arnold Weimerskirch. *Total Quality Management.* New York: John Wiley, 1994.

Editors of *Business Week. The Quality Imperative.* New York: McGraw-Hill, 1994.

European Quality. "Beyond Benchmarking." *Quality Digest,* June 1994, pp. 22–28.

Hiebler, Robert. "A Roadmap for Success." *Industry Week,* July 19, 1993, p. 53.

Kinni, Theodore B. "Benchmarking." *Quality Digest,* November 1993, pp. 24–29.

McGonagle, John J. and Denise Fleming. "New Options in Benchmarking." *Journal for Quality and Participation,* July/August 1993, pp. 60–67.

McCloskey, Larry A. and Dennis N. Collett, *TQM: A Basic Text.* Methuen, MA: Goal/QPC, 1993.

Sashkin, Marshall and Kenneth J. Kiser. *Putting Total Quality Management to Work.* San Francisco: Berrett-Koehler Publishers, 1993.

Sheridan, John. "Where Benchmarkers Go Wrong." *Industry Week,* March 15, 1993, pp. 28–34.

QUALITY AND BENCHMARKING REFERENCES (continued)

Watson, Gregory H. *Strategic Benchmarking*. New York: John Wiley, 1993.

Younger, Sandra Miller. *Understanding Benchmarking: The Search for Best Practices.* Alexandria, VA: ASTD, 1992.

Associations and Other Sources of Help

American Productivity and Quality Center (APQC). 123 North Post Oak Lane, Houston, Texas 77024. Telephone: 713-681-4020.
This is the group that has the International Benchmarking Clearinghouse.

American Society for Quality Control (ASQC). Box 3005, Milwaukee, Wisconsin 53201. Telephone: 800-248-1946.
The world's number one quality organization.
(Ninth in a series of annual surveys conducted for ASQC, The Gallup Organization conducted telephone interviews with 1,293 full-time employed adults during July 1993. Single copies of the survey summary (item T733) are available free of charge. For more information, call ASQC at 800-248-1946.)

Association for Quality and Participation (AQP). 801-B West 8th Street, Cincinnati, Ohio 45203. Telephone: 513-381-1959.

On-line Resources

The Benchmarking Exchange. Telephone: 800-662-9801.

Quality On-line Forum. Telephone: 913-234-6528 or 913-379-5590 for more information.

TQM BBS. A free BBS. With your modem, call 301-585-1164.

Internet Resources

The internet offers you a wealth of quality and benchmarking information sources. You can access the internet through providers like CompuServe, Prodigy, and American Online. Or, you can use other national internet providers. For more information, check the business page of your local newspaper. Some companies provide software. You can use a third-party software such as Spry's top-rated "Internet in a Box 2.0," available in many software stores.

World Wide Web (WWW) Pages of Interest

Organization	*URL Address*
American Quality and Productivity Center and International Benchmarking Clearinghouse	http://www.apqc.org/
American Society for Quality Control	http://www.asqc.org
The Benchmarking Exchange	http://www.benchnet.com/
British Quality Network	http://www.quality.co.uk
Demining Network from Clemson University	http://deming.eng.clemson.edu
ISO Online	http://www.iso.ch/welcome.html
Quality Resources On-Line	http://www.quailty.org:80/qc/
The Quality Wave	http://www.xnet.com/~creacib/Q4Q/

Usenet Groups of Interest

misc.industry.quality

bit.listserv.quality

To update this list, including information on the latest quality mailing lists, you can subscribe to *Quality Digest.* For a copy of their March 1995 "Cruising the Internet" article, e-mail them at qualitydg@aol.com or fax them at 916–527–6983.

QUALITY AND BENCHMARKING REFERENCES (continued)

Quality Award Programs

Many US states administer quality awards. Check with ASQC to find out the address and phone number of the award program in your state.

In addition, there are several national and international quality award programs you should consider:

The Malcolm Baldrige National Quality Award, US Department of Commerce, N.I.S.T., Route 270 and Quince Orchard Road, Room A537, Gaithersburg, Maryland 20899. Telephone: 301-975-2036 or FAX: 301-948-3716.
Learning the 7 categories and 24 items of the award will give you ideas on what important processes you need to benchmark in your organization. Call or write for an in-depth explanation of the criteria and an application blank.

The Shingo Prize for Excellence in Manufacturing, College of Business, Utah State University, Logan, Utah 84322. Telephone: 801-797-2279.

The RIT/USA Today Quality Cup, Carol Ann Skalski, Quality Cup, USA Today, 1000 Wilson Blvd., 22nd Floor, Arlington, Virginia 22229. Telephone: 703-276-5890.

The Deming Prize. Kohei Suzue, President, the Union of Japanese Scientists and Engineers, 5-10-11 Sendagaya, Shibuya-ku, Tokyo 151 Japan.

The European Quality Cup, The European Foundation for Quality Management, Avenue des Pleiades 19, B-1200 Brussels, Belgium.

International Benchmarking Award, which is awarded by the IBC of the American Productivity and Quality Center.

THE MALCOLM BALDRIGE NATIONAL QUALITY AWARD CRITERIA

You can use the criteria, values and categories of the Baldrige to benchmark your critical processes against the best.

The award program is designed to strengthen US competitiveness three ways:

1. To help improve performance practices and capabilities

2. To facilitate communication and sharing of best practices information among and within organizations of all types based upon a common understanding of key performance requirements

3. To serve as a working tool for managing performance, planning, training, and assessment

Award Criteria

The award criteria are built around the following core values and concepts:

- Customer-Driven Quality

- Leadership

- Continuous Improvement and Learning

- Employee Participation and Development

- Fast Response Cycles

- Design Quality and Waste Prevention

- Long-Range View of the Future

- Management by Fact, Not Emotion

- Internal/External Partnership Development

- Corporate Responsibility and Citizenship

- Results Orientation

THE MALCOLM BALDRIGE NATIONAL QUALITY AWARD CRITERIA

The Four Elements

The seven categories are tied together by a framework of four elements:

The *"Driver"* (Category 1.0) is leadership that sets directions, creates values, goals, and systems, and guides the pursuit of customer value and company performance improvement.

The *"System"* (Categories 2.0, 3.0, 4.0 and 5.0) is made up of a set of well-defined and well-designed processes for meeting the company's customer and performance requirements.

The *"Measures of Progress"* (Category 6.0) provides a results-oriented basis for channeling actions to delivering ever-improving customer value and company performance. These areas include:

- Product and Service Quality

- Productivity Improvement

- Waste Reduction and Elimination

- Supplier Performance

- Financial Results

The *"Goal"* (Category 7.0) is the delivery of ever-improving value to customers and success in the marketplace. This includes: customer satisfaction, customer satisfaction relative to competitors, customer retention, and market share gain.

1995 BALDRIGE AWARD EXAMINATION CRITERIA—ITEM LISTING

Categories/Items	Point Values
1.0 Leadership	**90 Points Total**
1.1 Senior Executive Leadership	45
1.2 Leadership System and Organization	25
1.3 Public Responsibility and Corporate Citizenship	20
2.0 Information and Analysis	**75 Points Total**
2.1 Management of Information and Data	20
2.2 Competitive Comparisons and Benchmarking	15
2.3 Analysis and Use of Company-Level Data	40
3.0 Strategic Planning	**55 Points Total**
3.1 Strategy Development	35
3.2 Strategy Deployment	20
4.0 Human Resource Development and Management	**140 Points Total**
4.1 Human Resource Planning and Evaluation	20
4.2 High Performance Work Systems	45
4.3 Employee Education, Training, and Development	50
4.4 Employee Well-Being and Satisfaction	25
5.0 Process Management	**140 Points Total**
5.1 Design and Introduction of Products and Services	40
5.2 Process Management: Product and Service Production and Delivery	40
5.3 Process Management: Support Services	30
5.4 Management of Supplier Performance	30
6.0 Business Results	**250 Points Total**
6.1 Product and Service Quality Results	75
6.2 Company Operational and Financial	130
6.3 Supplier Performance Results	45
7.0 Customer Focus and Satisfaction	**250 Points Total**
7.1 Customer and Market Knowledge	30
7.2 Customer Relationship Management	30
7.3 Customer Satisfaction Determination	30
7.4 Customer Satisfaction Results	100
7.5 Customer Satisfaction Comparison	60

TOTAL POINTS = 1000

NOTES

NOTES

NOTES

NOTES

NOTES

NOW AVAILABLE FROM CRISP PUBLICATIONS

Books • Videos • CD Roms • Computer-Based Training Products

If you enjoyed this book, we have great news for you. There are over 200 books available in the *50-Minute*™ Series. To request a free full-line catalog, contact your local distributor or Crisp Publications, Inc., 1200 Hamilton Court, Menlo Park, CA 94025. Our toll-free number is 800-422-7477.

Subject Areas Include:

Management

Human Resources

Communication Skills

Personal Development

Marketing/Sales

Organizational Development

Customer Service/Quality

Computer Skills

Small Business and Entrepreneurship

Adult Literacy and Learning

Life Planning and Retirement

CRISP WORLDWIDE DISTRIBUTION

English language books are distributed worldwide. Major international distributors include:

ASIA/PACIFIC

Australia/New Zealand: In Learning, PO Box 1051 Springwood QLD, Brisbane, Australia 4127
Telephone: 7-841-1061, Facsimile: 7-841-1580
ATTN: Mssrs. Gordon

Singapore: Graham Brash (Pvt) Ltd. 32, Gul Drive, Singapore 2262
Telphone: 65-861-1336, Facsimile: 65-861-4815
ATTN: Mr. Campbell

EUROPEAN UNION

England: Flex Training, Ltd. 9-15 Hitchin Street, Baldock, Hertfordshire, SG7 6AL
Telephone: 1-462-896000, Facsimile: 1-462-892417
ATTN: Mr. Willets

INDIA

Multi-Media HRD, Pvt., Ltd., National House, Tulloch Road, Appolo Bunder, Bombay, India 400-039
Telephone: 91-22-204-2281, Facsimile: 91-22-283-6478
ATTN: Mssrs. Aggarwal

MIDDLE EAST

United Arab Emirates: Al-Mutanabbi Bookshop, PO Box 71946, Abu Dhabi
Telephone: 971-2-321-519, Facsimile: 971-2-317-706

NORTH AMERICA

Canada: Reid Publishing, Ltd., Box 69559-109 Thomas Street, Oakville, Ontario Canada L6J 7R4.
Telephone: (905) 842-4428, Facsimile: (905) 842-9327

SOUTH AMERICA

Mexico: Grupo Editorial Iberoamerica, Serapio Rendon #125, Col. San Rafael, 06470 Mexico, D.F.
Telephone: 525-705-0585, Facsimile: 525-535-2009
ATTN: Señor Grepe

SOUTH AFRICA

Alternative Books, Unit A3 Sanlam Micro Industrial Park, Hammer Avenue STRYDOM Park, Randburg, 2194 South Africa
Telephone: 2711 792 7730, Facsimile: 2711 792 7787
ATTN: Mr. de Haas

Selected Crisp titles are available in 23 languages. For more information contact International Publishing Manager, Suzanne Kelly-Lyall at (415) 323-6100.